Table of Contents

Animals in Danger

Animals around the world are in great danger. One reason is because people have taken over the land these animals call home. Without space to find food or shelter, animals may become **endangered**. Other factors include **pollution**, disease, and the over-hunting of a **species**.

endangered at risk of dying out

pollution harmful materials that damage the air, water and soil

species group of plants or animals that share common features

4

First Facts®

The Most Endangered ANIMALS IN THE WORLD

by Tammy Gagne

Raintree is an imprint of Capstone Global Library Limited, a company incorporated in England and Wales having its registered office at 7 Pilgrim Street, London, EC4V 6LB – Registered company number: 6695582

www.raintree.co.uk
myorders@raintree.co.uk

Editorial Credits
Kathryn Clay, editor; Bobbie Nuytten, designer; Jo Miller, media researcher; Kathy McColley, production specialist

ISBN 978 1 4062 9308 1 (hardback)
18 17 16 15 14
10 9 8 7 6 5 4 3 2 1

ISBN 978 1 4062 9312 8 (paperback)
19 18 17 16 15
10 9 8 7 6 5 4 3 2 1

British Library Cataloguing in Publication Data
A full catalogue record for this book is available from the British Library.

Photo Credits
Corel, cover (bottom right); Getty Images: National Geographic/Roy Toft, 9, 22; Newscom: Design Pics/Dave Fleetham, 17, 22, VWPics/Francois Gohier, 7, 22, ZUMA Press/Photoshot/ Evolve, 5, 22; Shutterstock: Bakalusha, 6, Bildagentur Zoonar GmbH, 15, 22, FloridaStock, 4, guentermanaus, 10, Jean-Edouard Rozey, cover (bottom left), Kletr, 16, Matt Gibson, 11, 22, Monika Hrdinova, cover (top), 1, 22, Photodynamic, 13, Slateterreno, cover (middle), wormig, 22 (map); SuperStock: John Warburton Lee, 19, 22, Minden Pictures, 21, 22

Fact: Red wolves are just one type of endangered animal. They once roamed the southern part of the United States. Today, only about 100 red wolves live in the wild.

North Atlantic Right Whale

North Atlantic right whales are among the rarest sea creatures in the world. Killing this species is illegal today. But many whales die when they get caught in fishing nets. Others die when they swim into ships. With only 350 still living, the species may soon become **extinct**.

extinct no longer existing; an extinct animal is one that has died out, with no more of its kind

Fact: North Atlantic right whale babies are called calves. They measure 4 to 4.5 metres (13 to 15 feet) when they are born.

Pygmy Raccoon

Pygmy raccoons look similar to other raccoons, but they are smaller and have golden tails. This species is found only on the island of Cozumel, off the south-east coast of Mexico. Illness is among the top threats to their survival. Stray cats and dogs have brought deadly diseases such as **rabies** to the island. Fewer than 500 pygmy raccoons are left in the wild.

rabies deadly disease that people and animals can get from the bite of an infected animal

Fact: Pygmy raccoons are also called Cozumel raccoons and dwarf raccoons.

Jaguar

The jaguar has lost much of its **habitat** over time. People have cut down the forests where these large cats live. Hunting has also decreased their numbers. The species used to live in both the south-western United States and Central and South America. About 15,000 jaguars are left today, mostly in South America.

habitat natural place and conditions in which an animal or plant lives

Fact: The jaguar is the third largest cat in the world today. Only the tiger and lion are larger.

Mountain Gorilla

About 700 mountain gorillas live in central Africa today. Many others have been the victims of hunting and human wars. Ongoing fighting in Rwanda, Uganda and the Congo makes saving the species especially difficult. Hunting mountain gorillas is illegal. But **poachers** continue to kill these animals.

poacher someone who hunts or fishes illegally

Fact: Baby mountain gorillas ride on their mothers' backs after they are about 4 months old. They continue riding up to the age of three.

Northern Sportive Lemur

The northern sportive lemur is the most endangered lemur in Madagascar. Only about 20 of these animals live on the island today. Farmers who burn land to grow crops have caused the lemur's habitat to shrink. This burning of land is thought to make the soil richer. But it destroys the homes of many animals.

Fact: About 100 different lemur species live in Madagascar. Like the northern sportive lemur, many of them are endangered.

Hawaiian Monk Seal

About 1,100 Hawaiian monk seals are left in the wild. Many are killed when they get caught in fishing nets. But some members of this endangered species are being killed by their own kind. Scientists have discovered that groups of males sometimes attack females. This practice is called mobbing.

Fact: Hawaiian monk seals do not fear people like many other wild animals do. They will not flee when a person approaches them.

17

Pygmy Tarsier

Too much attention can be a bad thing. This is the case with the pygmy tarsier in Indonesia. Tourists are drawn to this endangered species. But when people get too close, these animals become extremely tense. As a result they often bang their heads so hard that they die. To protect the tarsiers, tourists are now taught to stay away from the animals.

Fact: For more than 80 years, the pygmy tarsier was thought to be extinct. But in 2008, members of the species were found again on an island in Indonesia.

Kakapo Parrot

The kakapo parrot from New Zealand is the only parrot that cannot fly. Cats and rats have hunted this unique species to near extinction. Because it cannot fly, this species has difficulty getting away from **predators**. Fewer than 150 kakapo parrots are left in the wild today. Members of the Kakapo Recovery Programme and other groups work to increase the population of this endangered species.

predator animal that hunts other animals for food

Fact: So few kakapo parrots exist that researchers have given almost all of them names.

Habitat Map

North America

Europe

Asia

Africa

South America

Australia

North Atlantic Right Whale	Northern Sportive Lemur
Hawaiian Monk Seal	Kakapo Parrot
Red Wolf	Pygmy Tarsier
Pygmy Raccoon	Jaguar
	Mountain Gorilla

Glossary

endangered at risk of dying out

extinct no longer existing; an extinct animal is one that has died out, with no more of its kind

habitat natural place and conditions in which an animal or plant lives

poacher someone who hunts or fishes illegally

pollution harmful materials that damage the air, water and soil

predator animal that hunts other animals for food

rabies deadly disease that people and animals can get from the bite of an infected animal

species group of plants or animals that share common features

Comprehension Questions

1. How do pygmy raccoons differ from other raccoons?

2. Reread page 4 about how animals become endangered. What can people do to keep animals from becoming endangered?

Books

Animals in Danger in Europe (Animals in Danger), Richard and Louise Spilsbury (Raintree, 2014)

Endangered Animals (Eyewitness), Ben Hoare and Thomas Jackson (Dorling Kindersley, 2010)

Jaguar (A Day in the Life: Rainforest Animals), Anita Ganeri (Raintree, 2011)

Websites

http://gowild.wwf.org.uk
Learn about the physical features, habitats and behaviours of endangered animals from around the world.

http://www.ngkids.co.uk/did-you-know/Jaguar-facts
Learn 10 jaguar facts and view pictures of the jaguar.

Index